ORIGINS

WHODUNNIT

Organized Crime

C.M. Johnson

full tilt PRESS

Organized Crime
Origins: Whodunnit

Copyright © 2017
Published by Full Tilt Press
Written by C.M. Johnson
All rights reserved.

Full Tilt Press
42982 Osgood Road
Fremont, CA 94539
www.readfulltilt.com

Full Tilt Press publications may be purchased for educational, business, or sales promotional use.

Editorial Credits
Design and layout by Sara Radka
Edited by Lauren Dupuis-Perez
Copyedited by Renae Gilles

Image Credits
Getty Images: 6, 36, EyeEm, 41, iStockphoto, 1, 4, 11, 24, 44, Vetta, 14; Newscom: EPA, 12,
Everett Collection, 1, 34, Fotogramma/Splash News, 43, Pictures From History, 27, World
History Archive, 39, ZUMA Press, 33; Shutterstock: Claude Beaubien, 11, Dalshe, 26, davidk,
19, dikobraziy, 38, ESB Professional, 23, 41, Everett Historical, 17, 18, 20, Felix Mizioznikov, 10,
ID1974, 13, Katoosha, 21, Kobby Dagan, 40, Leon Rafael, 29, Lisovskaya Natalia, 31, Littleaom,
35, Maxim Tupikov, 28, mTaira, 30, NEstudio, 9, Paul Vasarhelyi, 7, Romasan, 25, Sebastian
Duda, 8; Vecteezy: background and cover elements; Wikimedia: 16, 37, Goldshtein G., 5

ISBN: 978-1-62920-614-1 (library binding)
ISBN: 978-1-62920-626-4 (eBook)

Printed in the United States of America.

Contents

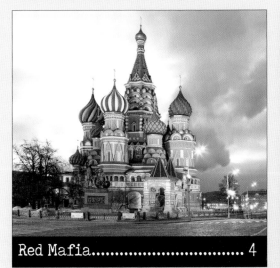

Red Mafia.............................. 4

Triads................................... 14

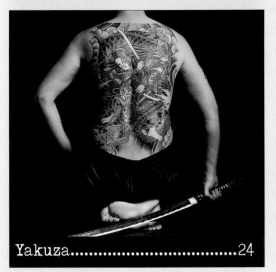

Yakuza................................24

Italian Mafia 34

Conclusion.............................44
Glossary...............................45
Quiz....................................46
Index..................................47
Selected Bibliography.........48

RED MAFIA

Though Russia has a long history of war and hardship, the country is also known for its rich tradition of art and culture.

Introduction

In the early 1900s, Russia was in chaos. The people wanted to **overthrow** their government, which led to a lot of violence and fighting. Then, in 1922, Russia became part of the Soviet Union. The new leaders kept control by creating fear. People who spoke up against them were sent to jail. At times, people were jailed for no reason at all. The Soviet Union was also poor. **Poverty** and fear made many people turn to crime. When criminals joined forces, a web of crime was born. This became the Russian, or Red, Mafia.

In 1917, Vladimir Lenin led an overthrow of the Russian Empire that led to the creation of the Soviet Union.

In the 1970s, the Red Mafia made its way to the United States. It started when some Jewish people left the Soviet Union because they were not allowed to practice their religion freely. The United States took them in as **refugees**. Others in the Soviet Union saw a chance for freedom. Some criminals in the Soviet Union saw a chance to get away as well. Whether or not they were Jewish, they stole the ID papers of Russian Jews who had died. They then escaped to the United States. With them came the Red Mafia.

DID YOU KNOW?

Before the Russian Empire was overthrown in 1917, the country was ruled by a royal family of male czars and female czarinas for almost 200 years.

overthrow: to remove from power

poverty: the state of being poor

refugee: a person who has been forced to leave their country because of war or for religious or political reasons

The wave of Soviet immigrants in the 1970s and '80s brought young families to Brighton Beach, New York, as well as businesses, such as restaurants and bookstores.

Red Mafia in Action

In the 1970s and '80s, Russian **immigrants** settled in an area of Brooklyn, New York, called Brighton Beach. Many came from a Soviet town called Odessa. Soon, Brighton Beach was called "Odessa by the Sea." Odessa had a history of crime, and some of the new arrivals were carrying on this tradition. Some stole jewels. Some **forged** papers. Some took money from other immigrants by threatening them. This is a crime called extortion.

immigrant: a person who comes to live in a different country than they were born in

forge: to illegally create or change a document

Most of these crimes were small. But in the early 1980s, Evsei Agron hit it big. Agron called himself the "godfather" of the Red Mafia. He started a gasoline **racket**. Agron bought large amounts of home heating oil, which was not taxed. He sold it as diesel fuel, which was taxed. Then he kept the tax money. This scheme made him and other Russian crooks rich. They gained power in the crime worlds of New York and New Jersey.

For a while, Agron's scam worked well. He bought expensive clothes. He ate at fancy clubs. Then other crooks began to take notice. Some were rivals in the Red Mafia. Others were in the Italian-American Mafia. Both wanted in on the scam, but they did not want to share the money with Agron. It would be easier if he were dead. In 1984, Agron was shot, though he did not die. The next year, two men posing as joggers went after him again. When Agron stepped out of his apartment, they shot him. This time, he died from his wounds.

racket: a business that makes money through illegal or dishonest activities

Crooks like Evsei Agron kept tax money, instead of giving it to the government. This is called tax evasion.

History of Crime

The Red Mafia rose out of Soviet Union prisons in the early 1900s and is said to be gaining power.

1922

Russia becomes part of the Soviet Union. A criminal underworld grows in jails and forced labor camps called gulags.

Early 1980s

In Brooklyn, Evsei Agron begins his gasoline racket. It costs the United States $1 billion a year in lost tax dollars.

1985

Agron is shot dead in Park Slope, Brooklyn. Police think that one of the families in the Italian-American Mafia is involved. But the murderers are never arrested.

1986

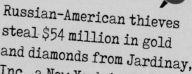

Russian-American thieves steal $54 million in gold and diamonds from Jardinay, Inc., a New York jeweler.

1991

The Soviet Union breaks up. Former members of the Soviet military join the Red Mafia in Brooklyn, bringing automatic weapons with them.

1990

Peter Grenenko retires. He was the only Russian-speaking detective in New York City's police department. His retirement makes it harder for police to get tips from Russian-Americans about crime in their community.

1995

Vyacheslav Ivankov, the leading Russian criminal in the United States, is arrested. He was trying to extort millions of dollars from two kidnapped businessmen in Miami, Florida.

2015

The *International Business Times* reports that the Red Mafia has gained strength in Ukraine, where gangs are bringing illegal weapons and drugs.

2016

Mark Galeotti at *Newsweek* says that the Red Mafia is returning to power. This reporter writes that Vladimir Putin, the Russian president, wants Russia to be a "superpower of crime."

Sunny Isles Beach, a neighborhood in Miami, has so many Russian-Americans that it is known as "Little Moscow." Moscow is the capital of Russia.

To Help or to Harm?

Many Red Mafia **mobsters** are well-educated. Their scams are clever. Talented artists make fake copies of great art. They pretend the pieces are the real thing and sell them at high prices. Tech wizards cheat credit card companies. In the 1980s, the Red Mafia helped make Brighton Beach rich. They did the same in the Russian neighborhoods of Miami, Florida, and Los Angeles, California. Home prices went up. Cafés and shops did well because people had money to spend. People like Ben Letterman were happy. In 1990, Letterman was the director of the Brighton Beach Business Improvement District. He said that the Red Mafia kept street crime down. Letterman didn't think they were bad people. He thought that the Mafia's dishonest deals were just like many done by bankers on Wall Street.

mobster: a member of a criminal gang

Other Russian-Americans are afraid of the Red Mafia. Many say the Russian Mafia brings violence and fear to Russian-American neighborhoods. In the 1970s and '80s, one gangster carried an electric cattle prod to scare people into giving him money. The Red Mafia has been known to pick on those who are afraid of the police. They also look for people who do not speak English, knowing these people will find it difficult to go to the police for help.

There are an estimated 700,000 Russian-Americans living in New York City. Many are concentrated in the neighborhood of Brighton Beach.

ART SCAM

One Russian art scam involved the famous Fabergé eggs. In 1885, the Russian emperor Alexander III gave his wife a gold egg at Easter. It was made by the artist Peter Carl Fabergé. Alexander began a royal family tradition of giving eggs made of gold and jewels as gifts. It continued until the end of the empire in 1917.

In November 2010, 354 bejeweled eggs arrived at the Paris airport. They had been sent from Russia. They were going to be sold during the Christmas season. They were marked as valuable Fabergé eggs from the 1800s, but French officials were suspicious and opened the package. They discovered it had been sent by Russian crooks. Officials said the eggs inside were lovely, but they were also fake.

Vladimir Putin has been the president of Russia since 2000.

The Red Mafia Today

In 1990, US officials did not think of the Red Mafia as true organized crime. They said the crooks had only loose ties to each other. The criminals fought with one another. Only a few people were in on each scam. Other organized crime groups worked better as a team. US officials said the real crime rings were from Italy and China. The New York police disagreed with this view. They said the Red Mafia was fierce. It was secretive. Quietly, the Red Mafia was piling up big sums of money. More money would mean more power.

DID YOU KNOW?

In 2016, officials in Germany said that Russian hackers, possibly working with President Putin, made a **cyberattack** on German computer systems.

In 1994, Russian president Boris Yeltsin said he feared for his country. He said it would soon be a "superpower of crime." Today, many crime experts say that Yeltsin's fear is coming true. They say that the current Russian president, Vladimir Putin, seems to be working with criminals, and that he uses secret violence and threats. In early 2006, Alexander Litvinenko made a report about Putin. Litvinenko had used to work for the president. He quit because he said Putin was dishonest and a killer. He said Putin had ties to crime gangs. Did this anger Putin?

Litvinenko thought so. A few months later, Litvinenko became ill in London. Police believed someone poisoned his tea. Before he died, Litvinenko said Putin had put out a **hit** on him.

cyberattack: an attempt by electronic hackers to destroy or disrupt a computer system

hit: an order to kill someone

Alexander Litvinenko's friend wore a mask when they spoke publicly about Putin's brutal ways. Many Russians believe covering their faces will protect them from the leader's possible revenge.

TRIADS

The early Triads hated the Qing dynasty, and wanted China's previous leaders, the Ming dynasty, to take power again. They wrote secret texts that contained the verse, "We shall overthrow the Qing and restore the Ming."

Introduction

In 1644, the Qing dynasty took over China. Soon, a secret group was formed: the Triads. These **rebels** wanted to get rid of the Qings. Around the same time, drugs became a problem in China. In 1650, the Dutch began to sell opium there. Many people became addicted. In 1729, the drug was banned. The Triads saw this as an opportunity to make money. They began **smuggling** drugs into China. They were good at it. They could work without being noticed. They had secret codes. They had rules and strong leaders. This made them well-organized.

In 1860, after several years of war, Great Britain and France forced China to make opium legal again. The Chinese government was weakened by these wars. It could not control the Triads, and the secret societies took over much of the opium trade.

The drug opium is made from the milky fluid in the seed pod of a poppy plant.

DID YOU KNOW?

In 1839, while opium was still illegal in China, Chinese officials destroyed more than 20,000 chests of opium imported illegally into China by British merchants.

rebel: a person who opposes or works against those in power

smuggle: to bring something from one place to another illegally

Early Chinese immigrants in the United States opened many types of businesses before anti-Chinese laws stopped them from doing certain jobs.

Triads in Action

In the 1800s, about 300,000 Chinese immigrants came to the United States. Some came to mine for gold. Others opened shops. A few were Triad members. In the United States, groups of Triad members were called Tongs. "Tong" means a hall or gathering place. Some of these Tong societies set up gambling rings. Others sold drugs. The drugs were often sent to them from the Triads in China. The Triads had a large supply of opium. There are three countries near China that have many poppy farms. These countries—Thailand, Laos, and Myanmar—are known as the "Golden Triangle."

In the 1960s and '70s, the Triads grew. The United States was fighting a war in Vietnam, which borders China. Opium was easy to get. Many US troops used it. In 1973, the United States left the war. Some troops went home. Others went to Europe. Wherever they went, the Triads went, too. They had more drugs to sell. They figured out ways to get drugs into US and European cities. They found people to sell and deliver the drugs there. They began to sell to locals, too. Triad members became rich. They also gained more power. Soon, the Triads had **contacts** all over the world.

contact: a person who you know and who can be helpful to you, especially in business

Many Chinese men came to the United States without their wives, hoping to get rich and return to China. In New York City's Chinatown in the late 1800s and early 1900s, men outnumbered women about 200 to 1.

History of Crime

The Triads have existed as a secret society since the 1640s. Today, they supply illegal drugs to much of the world.

1602–1683

The Dutch sell an average of 12.7 tons (11.5 metric tons) of opium per year to China.

1644

The Triads start as a rebel political group during the Qing dynasty.

1729

Drug addiction is a big problem in China. The emperor outlaws opium. The Triads begin to smuggle it in illegally.

1909

The United States bans smoking opium. In the same year, a "Tong war" between two Triad gangs claims 350 lives in New York.

1947

Mao Zedong and his communist forces take power in China. Mao cracks down on the opium trade. Triad members flee to Hong Kong, a British colony in southeastern China. They create a criminal network there.

1965

New immigration laws are passed in the United States. Many boys and young men come from Hong Kong. Some join Tong gangs in New York City, Chicago, Boston, and San Francisco.

1988

Federal agents raid the Chicago headquarters of a Tong gang named On Leong. They find evidence of On Leong's large crime network.

2013

In Hong Kong, police arrest 1,800 Triad members on charges of illegal gambling and drug offenses.

2013

US officials estimate that the Triads smuggle in 100,000 illegal immigrants from China into the United States every year. The immigrants are forced to work for the Triads to pay off debts.

In 1848, nuggets of gold were found in the Sacramento Valley in California. Many people in China came to the United States to try to strike it rich.

To Help or to Harm?

When the Chinese came to the United States in the 1800s, they faced **hostility**. The Chinese worked in mines. They helped build railroads. But they were not paid as much as white workers. They were also blamed whenever the pay was lowered for other workers. During that time, Chinese immigrants were the victims of many violent crimes.

hostility: a deeply felt hatred, often accompanied by conflict or violence

MARTIAL ARTS

As in most organized crime rings, women are rare in the Triads. But boys as young as 10 work for the gangs. In Hong Kong, they are trained in martial arts schools. In the 1980s, the Triads owned nearly all of these schools. Recruits were trained there, then sent out onto the streets to fight. In the 1990s, many of these boys went on to act as extras in kung fu movies. Today, many Hong Kong gyms are owned by non-Triads. They hope to link the martial arts with fitness rather than crime.

Some places passed laws against the Chinese. They could not live in some neighborhoods, so many of them formed Chinatowns instead. Tong members often became leaders in these areas. They helped people open shops. They spoke for their neighbors in court. Some Tong members found legal jobs. However, this was not easy. Some cities kept the Chinese from working certain types of jobs. They did not have many choices. Some Tong members turned to crime. They terrorized Chinatowns by making shop owners pay for protection from thugs. If an owner did not pay, they beat him up. Some Tong members formed gangs. These were made up of boys who worked for the Tong leader. In return, the leader would teach the boys martial arts. Many Tong members were skilled fighters who had learned these arts in China.

The Triads Today

In 1947, China cracked down on drugs. Anyone who bought, sold, or grew opium was shot. Many Triads fled to Hong Kong, because China did not rule that British colony. By the 1960s, the Triads had a lot of power in Hong Kong. They had 20,000–30,000 members. In parts of the colony, the British did not enforce the law. Triad gangs like Sun Yee On and 14K worked openly. They ran the drug business.

> **DID YOU KNOW?**
>
> Crime ruled in Kowloon Walled City, Hong Kong, from the 1950s until 1994. This city included about 33,000 residents living in 300 buildings on a single city block.

Today, the Triads still sell drugs. They have dealers all over the world. But they are less visible in Hong Kong. In 1997, China got control of the colony back from Great Britain. Chinese police worked **undercover** to go after the Triads. They have had a big effect.

Today, the Triads don't hold gang **initiations** or use secret codes anymore. These might get them caught. Members do not know who to trust. Anyone could be an undercover police officer. This has weakened the Triads. Police have arrested more than 1,800 gang members. Other members have given up crime. They grew tired of sneaking around. Many have gone into legal jobs, such as banking and real estate.

undercover: working secretly to catch criminals or collect information

initiation: a ritual or ceremony in which people are officially made members of a society or gang

While Hong Kong was under British rule, Triad gangs in the colony ran extortion rings at nightclubs and even controlled bus routes. Today, they operate less openly.

YAKUZA

Yakuza members often get full-body tattoos called *irezumi*. The tattoos are done by hand, without an electric needle. To get a tattoo in this slow, painful way is a sign of bravery and toughness.

Introduction

The largest crime networks in the world are from Japan. They are called the Yakuza. The Yakuza are made up of gangs often based on family connections. Each family gang has a strict order. A central leader rules. This leader has a **deputy**, who rules other members. Members respect the authority of those above them.

Samurai valued skills in battle, but they also emphasized the importance of loyalty, honesty, and respect for one's elders.

The origins of the Yakuza are not clear. Some think they can be linked to the Japanese samurai. Samurai were warriors hired by rich landowners. They were experts in swordplay. They had strong codes of honor. In the early seventeenth century, things were peaceful in Japan. Some samurai found themselves without work. They roamed the countryside looking for jobs. Some were hired as assassins. Others became bandits. The samurai began forming gangs around a boss, called a *kumi-cho*. These gangs moved into cities. There, they began to take charge.

DID YOU KNOW?

The word *yakuza* means "good for nothing" and is thought to have come from the name for a bad hand in a Japanese card game.

deputy: a person who is second in command and is in charge when the boss is absent

Yakuza in Action

In Japan, it is not illegal to be in a Yakuza gang. Members mark the name of the gang they belong to on their office doors. For years, police and the Yakuza had a deal. As long as the gangs did not hurt **law-abiding** citizens, they were left alone. In exchange, the gangs controlled the illegal gambling and drug trades. They kept violence down. They kept the worst drugs off the streets.

law-abiding: following the law

The Yakuza run many illegal casinos in Japanese cities like Tokyo and Osaka.

In 1960, the Japanese government hired a security force made up of Yakuza members to protect a visiting foreign leader.

In the 1960s, things changed. Japan's economy grew. The Yakuza also made more money. They spread out to other countries. In the United States, they showed up in Hawaii. They went to China and South Korea. In Japan, they expanded into construction and real estate. When a company wanted to start a new building project, sometimes the people living on the property didn't want to move. Gangs were paid to scare them away. In the 1980s, the Yakuza bought hotels and golf courses. They made a lot of money and donated some of it to politicians. This gave the Yakuza political power. In 1987, Noboru Takeshita ran for prime minister of Japan. An **opposing** group was harassing him. Suddenly, the harassment stopped. Takeshita had gone to a Yakuza gang for help. The gang silenced the group, and Takeshita won the election.

opposing: in conflict with each other

History of Crime

The Yakuza's code of loyalty and respect for authority within their ranks goes back to the 1600s.

Early 1600s

Jobless samurai begin to form criminal gangs in urban areas of Japan.

1915

Yamaguchi Harukichi founds the Yamaguchi-gumi, which soon becomes the Yakuza's most powerful gang.

1939–1945

The Yamaguchi-gumi falls apart during World War II.

1946

In Kōbe, Japan, Taoka Kazuo begins rebuilding Yamaguchi-gumi. He gets the gang into the movie and music industries.

1972

Wataru "Jackson" Inada, a member of the Sumiyoshi-kai, the second-largest Yakuza crime family, moves from Tokyo to Hawaii. He connects with the Italian-American Mafia and starts smuggling drugs into the United States and guns into Japan.

2008

Yakuza member Tadamasa Goto makes a deal with the FBI to get a life-saving liver transplant in Los Angeles. In exchange, he gives up information about the Yakuza. Goto makes a $100,000 donation to the hospital and is voted out of Yamaguchi-gumi.

1984

A split in Yamaguchi-gumi causes several years of gang wars in Japan.

2012

President Barack Obama closes the bank accounts of two of the biggest Yakuza gangs in order to limit their activity in the United States.

2015

Yamaguchi-gumi again breaks up into two factions, sparking fears of another gang war.

The **2011** earthquake in Japan caused a tsunami, or giant ocean wave. Its 30-foot (9-meter) waves destroyed so many buildings that 5 million tons (4.5 million metric tons) of debris were swept offshore.

To Help or To Harm?

On March 11, 2011, an earthquake hit northeast Japan. Almost 16,000 people died. More than 300,000 lost their homes. The Yakuza sent trucks full of food and water. The aid was worth more than $500,000. They had done the same after an earthquake in 1995 in Kōbe. The Yakuza work efficiently. They often deliver aid faster than the government can. Manabu Miyazaki studies the Yakuza. He says that often, members are people who are **discriminated** against in Japan.

They are outcasts. They know what it is to suffer. They want to help people in trouble.

discriminate: to unfairly treat a person or group of people differently than other people or groups

BURAKUMIN

Many Yakuza members come from a group called "Burakumin." These are people whose families have traditionally worked as butchers, undertakers, and leather **tanners**. These trades are linked with death. The Burakumin continue to be shunned in Japan. Lists of Burakumin are circulated secretly. Companies use them to weed out job applicants. People also check the ancestry of their future husband or wife. In a 2014 survey in Tokyo, 1 out of 10 people said they would not want their child to marry someone from a Burakumin family.

Others say the Yakuza give aid only to help their image. It is true that the Yakuza pay attention to how they look to the public. Yakuza gangs run parts of Japan's film industry. In their films, the Yakuza are shown in a positive light. They are kind leaders. They do things to help people. The Yakuza also run talent agencies. If a singer or actor does not want to work at an agency, mob bosses often take it as an insult. In 2016, a former Yakuza member, Kazuo Kasaoka, stepped forward. He had worked at a big agency in Japan. But he left in 2005 after refusing to follow an order from his boss. The order was to kill an actress for ending her contract.

tanner: a person who turns animal skins into leather

The Yakuza Today

Today, the Yakuza are not as open as they once were. In the 1990s, the police did not like the Yakuza's new role in industry and politics. They felt the Yakuza had broken their original deal. They had harmed law-abiding citizens. It is still legal to be in a gang in Japan. But in 1992, a new law said the police could close down gang offices. In 2011, the law was expanded. It was now illegal for a company to have Yakuza ties. The new laws have hurt the Yakuza's image. Members no longer publicly admit to being Yakuza. But hiding it is not easy. Many have Yakuza tattoos. Others lack a pinky finger. Sometimes, members chop one off to **atone** for a mistake.

> **DID YOU KNOW?**
>
> New police measures have caused a decline in Yakuza membership in Japan, which is down from about 91,000 in 1991 to 53,000 in 2015.

US officials are also fighting the Yakuza. The gangs are still in Hawaii. Now, they are also in California. They sell guns from the United States on Japan's **black market**. Japan has strict gun control laws. A cheap gun can sell for $1,000 there. US officials have cut off many sources of Yakuza money. Still, the Yakuza have been able to move east, to Las Vegas, Nevada. There they have made ties with the Italian-American Mafia. What might these two groups be able to do together?

atone: to make up for doing something bad

black market: the trade in goods or services that are illegal

Yakuza members are known for having tattoos all over their bodies. Many businesses in Japan will not hire people who have them.

ITALIAN MAFIA

One of the most famous gangsters in the Italian-American Mafia was Al Capone. He was the "king" of organized crime in Chicago in the 1920s.

Introduction

A "Mafia" is a secret criminal society. "Mafiosos," the members of the society, do not trust authority. In early Sicily, people had reason to be distrustful. Sicily is an island off Italy's coast. For centuries, it was invaded by many different foreign armies. The Sicilians formed groups to protect themselves. In the 1800s, these groups were called *mafie*. They made deals with landowners. If the owners paid up, the *mafie* would guard them from whoever invaded next. Those who didn't pay, the *mafie* considered enemies.

These *mafie* grew into the Italian Mafia. They **fixed** elections. They did work for the Catholic Church. They lived by the code of *omertà*. This meant they never went to the police. If a Mafioso was wronged, he took his own revenge. In 1878, the Italian government went after the Mafia. Some members escaped to the United States. But many Italians did not find jobs there. People would not hire them. So mobsters put their crime skills to use in their new home.

Today on the island of Sicily, the Italian Mafia still forces many shops, restaurants, and hotels to pay protection money, called *pizzo*.

DID YOU KNOW?

The first Italian-American Mafia killing in the United States occurred in 1889, when Vincenzo Ottumvo was murdered in the middle of a card game in New Orleans, Louisiana.

fix: to change the outcome of something by illegal or dishonest methods

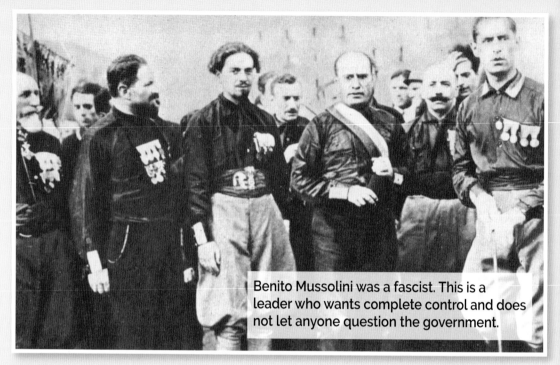

Benito Mussolini was a fascist. This is a leader who wants complete control and does not let anyone question the government.

Italian Mafia in Action

In 1920, Benito Mussolini rose to power in Italy. He drove more of the Mafia out. He wanted people to do as he said. He did not like this code of *omertà*.

The Mafia went to cities with Italian communities like New York City and Chicago. Small crime gangs were already there. They were about to get bigger. In 1919, the United States passed a law that enforced Prohibition. It was now illegal to make alcohol for drinking. However, alcohol could still be used in products such as hair oil. This gave the Mafia an idea. Gangs took over factories that made these types of products. They secretly made alcoholic beverages in these factories, too. Then they sold them all over the country.

In the 1920s, many people bought drinks in hidden bars. They had illegal drinks sent to their parties. Prohibition lasted for fourteen years. During that time, the Mafia made a lot of money. They used the money to **bribe** politicians and cops. They also connected with the public. Many people did not like Prohibition. They did not think drinking alcohol was wrong. To them, breaking the law made sense. Many people saw mobsters as heroes.

DID YOU KNOW?

In the 1920s, secret clubs where people drank alcohol illegally were called "speakeasies." There were thousands of these clubs in New York City and many more in other cities across the nation.

bribe: to offer money, goods, or services in order to get someone to do something

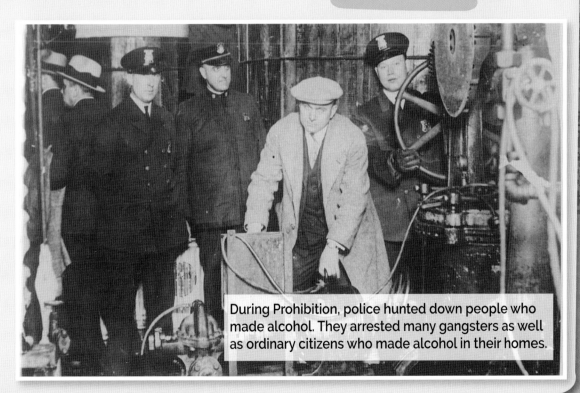

During Prohibition, police hunted down people who made alcohol. They arrested many gangsters as well as ordinary citizens who made alcohol in their homes.

History of Crime

The Italian Mafia has been active since the 1800s, and gained power in the United States in the 1920s.

1878

Many Mafiosos flee Italy when the government cracks down on organized crime.

1916

In New York City, a Mafia war begins between the Sicilians, who control Manhattan, and the Neapolitans, from Naples, Italy, who control Brooklyn.

1950–1951

The US Senate creates the Kefauver Committee to investigate organized crime.

1970

A new set of laws is passed in the United States. It is called the Racketeer Influenced and Corrupt Organizations Act (RICO). Investigators can now seek longer prison terms for criminals with Mafia connections.

1972

The movie *The Godfather* is released. It helps create a glamorous image of the rich, well-dressed Italian-American mobster.

1985

Paul Castellano, boss of the Gambino crime family, is murdered by John Gotti, who takes over.

1999-2007

HBO's TV show *The Sopranos* shows the sensitive side of an Italian-American mob boss named Tony Soprano. The character is often seen talking over his personal problems with a therapist.

2016

In Sicily, the gang Cosa Nostra makes big money from illegal horse races in the streets. Many horses are abused and killed.

By opening gambling clubs in Las Vegas, the Italian-American Mafia played a large part in turning the city into the popular tourist destination it is today.

To Help or to Harm?

At any given time, there are about 10 to 20 crime families in the Italian-American Mafia. In New York City, there are five. Cities like St. Louis, Missouri, and Las Vegas have one family each. Often, the families fight for power. They want in on every scam. They kill to keep and gain control.

In 1931, crime boss Salvatore Maranzano won a gang war. Afterward he claimed to be the "boss of all bosses." Rival mob boss Charles "Lucky" Luciano had Maranzano killed. Luciano then started the "Commission." This was a group of Mafia leaders. It was meant to stop power grabs. The Commission created rules. It **mediated** disputes. Members joined from across the country. But the Commission didn't stop the violence completely. In 1936, Chicago hitman Jack McGurn was shot dead while bowling. In 1957, Gambino family mob boss Albert Anastasia was killed in a barbershop in New York City. Luciano himself put out the hit. Anastasia had been trying to move in on a deal on casinos in Cuba.

mediate: to communicate or negotiate between two or more people or sides

In its early years, the Mafia gave to the poor. But the money often came from theft in their own communities. The mob has also often made Italian-American neighborhoods unsafe places. In 1926, a machine-gun attack on Al Capone killed an innocent person in Illinois. Mobsters also target people who fall on hard times. They loan people money and charge high **interest**. This is called loan sharking. The thugs threaten violence if a person can't pay.

Loan sharks often target gamblers who are deep in debt and have nowhere else to turn for help.

interest: a rate that is paid for the use of another person's money

THE "GENTLE DON"

Mob boss Angelo Bruno was called the "Gentle Don." A "don" refers to a powerful Mafia leader. Bruno's family was one of the most peaceful in the country. He ran scams in Philadelphia and New Jersey. In 1976, New Jersey voters approved casino gambling in Atlantic City. The Gambino family of New York wanted in. In 1978, the Gambino boss Paul Castellano came to New Jersey to make a deal with Bruno. The deal went bad. In 1980, Bruno was shot in his car. Dollar bills were found stuffed in his mouth to show that it was greed that killed him.

The Italian Mafia Today

In the 1950s, the Mafia in the United States ran scams in casinos and in the construction industry. They fixed races at dog tracks. They made millions. They were guilty of murder and assault. However, they rarely went to jail. Even rival bosses honored the code of *omertà*. They did not tell on one another. They also bribed judges and juries. If a juror did not accept a bribe, a mobster might issue a threat instead.

In 1970, things changed. US officials were fed up. Congress passed a law called the RICO Act. This let prosecutors cut off a gang's sources of money. They could also give long prison sentences to known mobsters, even if they were caught for small crimes. Soon, the code of *omertà* began to fail. When police offered deals to Mafiosos, they began to turn one another in.

Today, many US mob bosses are dead or in jail. But in Italy, the Mafia is doing well. The Camorra is the biggest gang there. They make about $4.9 billion a year. They sell guns. They run **counterfeiting** rings. Another gang, the 'Ndrangheta, supplies drugs to much of Europe. Recently, they have also become interested in US crime. They've started to help rebuild the Gambino and Bonanno families of New York.

> **DID YOU KNOW?**
>
> In the 1930s, at Al Capone's dog track in Illinois, all but one greyhound would be overfed before a race. This made the dogs sleepy and slow. The mob would bet all its money on the unfed dog.

counterfeiting: the process of making a fake copy of something of value

The Italian Mafia gang Camorra is still powerful in Naples, Italy, despite recent arrests of mob bosses. The gang often recruits unemployed teenagers and even children into its ranks.

Conclusion

What can an illegal business do if it is cheated? What if a customer does not pay? The owner can't go to the police. This is why organized crime has so much violence. Crime gangs must find ways to defend their interests. If they don't, they will go out of business.

Will we always have organized crime? To answer that question, we need to look at where it comes from. In the movie *Goodfellas*, the character of Henry Hill says that as a child, he dreamed of a life as a gangster. He wanted to be rich and tough. He wanted to outsmart the police. However, in real life, most people join crime gangs because they feel they do not have much of a choice. There are no jobs. Or no one will hire them because of their race. Most say that if they had better options, they would take them. The thrill of crime gets old when you always have to run from the police.

Glossary

atone: to make up for doing something bad

black market: the trade in goods or services that are illegal

bribe: to offer money, goods, or services in order to get someone to do something

contact: a person who you know and who can be helpful to you, especially in business

counterfeiting: the process of making a fake copy of something of value

cyberattack: an attempt by electronic hackers to destroy or disrupt a computer system

deputy: a person who is second in command and is in charge when the boss is absent

discriminate: to unfairly treat a person or group of people differently than other people or groups

fix: to change the outcome of something by illegal or dishonest methods

forge: to illegally create or change a document

hit: an order to kill someone

hostility: a deeply felt hatred, often accompanied by conflict or violence

immigrant: a person who comes to live in a different country than they were born in

initiation: a ritual or ceremony in which people are officially made members of a society or gang

interest: a rate that is paid for the use of another person's money

law-abiding: following the law

mediate: to communicate or negotiate between two or more people or sides

mobster: a member of a criminal gang

opposing: in conflict with each other

overthrow: to remove from power

poverty: the state of being poor

racket: a business that makes money through illegal or dishonest activities

rebel: a person who opposes or works against those in power

refugee: a person who has been forced to leave their country because of war or for religious or political reasons

smuggle: to bring something from one place to another illegally

tanner: a person who turns animal skins into leather

undercover: working secretly to catch criminals or collect information

Quiz

1 When did the Red Mafia start coming to the United States?

2 What is the name of the city in New York that is known for its large Russian community?

3 The Triads are an organized crime group that is originally from which country?

4 Today, how do the Triads make money?

5 The largest crime networks in the world are from which country?

6 How did the Yakuza help the people during the 2011 earthquake in Japan?

7 In what year did the Italian Mafia begin coming to the United States?

8 Who claimed to be "the boss of all bosses?"

8. Salvatore Maranzano

7. 1878

6. They sent trucks of food and water to victims.

5. Japan

4. By selling drugs

3. China

2. Brighton Beach

1. The 1970s

Index

Burakumin 31

Camorra 42, 43
Capone, Al 34, 41, 42
casinos. *See* gambling
Chicago, Illinois 19, 34, 36, 40

Fabergé eggs 11

gambling 16, 19, 26, 40, 41
Gotti, John 39

Hong Kong, China 19, 21, 22, 23

immigrants 6, 16, 19, 20
Ivankov, Vyacheslav 9

Las Vegas, Nevada 32, 40
Lenin, Vladimir 5
Letterman, Ben 10
Litvinenko, Alexander 13

martial arts 21
Mussolini, Benito 36

New York City, New York 9, 11, 17, 19, 36, 37, 38, 40

opium 15, 16, 17, 18, 19, 22

Prohibition 36, 37
Putin, Vladimir 9, 12, 13

Qing dynasty 14, 15, 18

samurai 25, 28
Sicily, Italy 35, 39
Soviet Union 5, 7, 8, 9

Takeshita, Noboru 27
tattoos 24, 32, 33
Tongs 16, 18, 19, 21

Yamaguchi-gumi 28, 29

Selected Bibliography

Abadinsky, Howard. *Organized Crime.* 6th Ed. Belmont, Calif.: Wadsworth, 2000.

Huston, Peter. *Tongs, Gangs, and Triads: Chinese Crime Groups in North America.* Boulder, Colo.: Paladin Press, 1995.

Sifakis, Carl. *The Mafia Encyclopedia: From Accardo to Zwillman.* New York: Facts on File, Inc., 2005.

Matthews, Chris. "Fortune 5: The Biggest Organized Crime Groups in the World." *FORTUNE.* Time Inc., September 13, 2014. Web. Accessed February 6, 2017. http://fortune.com/2014/09/14/biggest-organized-crime-groups-in-the-world/.

Rosenthal, James. "Russia's New Export the Mob." *The Washington Post.* June 24, 1990. Web. Accessed February 6, 2017. https://www.washingtonpost.com/archive/opinions/1990/06/24/russias-new-export-the-mob/6719d1b7-9fe9-4470-bb1f-f1fc452a986b.

"Opium Wars." *Encyclopædia Britannica Online.* Encyclopædia Britannica, n.d. Web. Accessed February 6, 2017. https://www.britannica.com/topic/Opium-Wars.

"Yakuza." *Encyclopædia Britannica Online.* Encyclopædia Britannica, n.d. Web. Accessed February 6, 2017. https://www.britannica.com/topic/yakuza/.

"Origins of the Mafia." *History.com.* A+E Networks, 2009. Web. Accessed February 6, 2017. http://www.history.com/topics/origins-of-the-mafia/.